CHAMPIONS!

CHAMPIONS!

THE STORY OF HOW THE TITLE WAS WON by Neil Plumb and Jon Sanders

CHAMPIONS!
THE STORY OF HOW THE TITLE WAS WON

Published By:
Pitch Publishing (Brighton) Ltd
A2 Yeoman Gate
Yeoman Way
Durrington
BN13 3QZ

Email: info@pitchpublishing.co.uk
Web: www.pitchpublishing.co.uk

First published 2009

A catalogue record for this book is available from the British Library.

10-digit ISBN: 1-9054117-2-3
13-digit ISBN: 978-1-9054117-2-6

Printed and bound in Malta by Gutenberg Press

Foreword by Nigel Pearson

I have had time to reflect on the season since the end of the campaign and I am very proud of what we achieved. I am also incredibly satisfied in the manner in which we went about the task that was put in front of us.

To win the League One title and gain promotion back to the Championship at the first attempt took a real team effort and every single person who was involved can take great pride out of what was accomplished. That obviously includes the fans. They travelled in great numbers to every game that was played up and down the land and I know for a fact that their support had a huge positive effect on the performances of the team on the pitch.

When I was handed the job of Leicester City manager I knew what was expected of me. I understood the requirements and I took on that responsibility. I was very grateful in the fact that I was able to compliment the excellent staff already at the club with Steve Walsh and Craig Shakespeare and with Milan's backing we were able to put together a team that we believed would allow us to reach our goal of promotion.

We never shied away from talking openly about our goal. Everybody knew what was expected of them and everyone rose to the challenge.

Neil Plumb, who took the photographs for this book, and Jon Sanders, who was at the time the club's press officer, were on the journey every step of the way and therefore well placed to capture and document every moment. They have put together a fantastic publication and I hope that you enjoy it as much as I have. It has certainly brought back some pleasant memories of what was an unforgettable campaign.

"Relegation was a bitter pill for us all to swallow, but we must now pick ourselves up off the floor and come back stronger than ever. Together we can make it happen."

Milan Mandaric (June 2008)

City's pre-season campaign got underway at the Marston's Stadium, home to Hinckley United. Ashley Chambers, pictured here with fellow Academy graduate James Wesolowski, grabbed the winning goal to clinch a 5-4 victory in what was a thoroughly entertaining opener.

There was no evidence of a relegation hangover on the terraces – with Foxes fans travelling in numbers to see Nigel Pearson's new look side in action. And the goals were certainly flowing on the pitch as City followed up their good start with an 8-4 victory at Quorn.

City put in arguably their finest performance of the pre-season campaign at Selhurst Park, where they were unlucky to only come away with a 1-1 draw against a strong Neil Warnock led outfit.

JAKO
Topps
Tiles
logistics
LCFC

Nigel Pearson's new recruits were on show at the club's annual photocall – with Michael Morrison, Lloyd Dyer, Nicky Adams, Alex Tunchev and Kerrea Gilbert all in attendance at the Walkers Stadium. Jack Hobbs and former striker Paul Dickov would further bolster Pearson's charges ahead of the big kick off.

Blue skies ahead.... Paul Dickov gave a real shot in the arm to the club when he signed on the dotted line ahead of the MK Dons fixture.

The Foxes got their season underway in style with a 2-0 victory over newly promoted MK Dons. Matty Fryatt got his campaign off to a flyer with a brace, while Max Gradel (right), Alex Tunchex, Michael Morrison, Lloyd Dyer and Kerrea Gilbert all made their full City debuts on the day.

After being overlooked for the majority of the pre-season campaign, Andy King found himself thrust in to the limelight in the Palace fixture. The youngster revelled in his new found status and was instrumental in City's fine start to the season.

Britannia
BUILDING SOCIETY
smile

The 2007-08 season had been one to forget for the Leicester City players – none more so than Matty Fryatt. However, those memories were a distant thing of the past as a Fryatt brace helped the Foxes to a 3-1 victory over Tranmere Rovers.

Topps
Tiles
O'CALLAGHAN
8

Coca-Cola FOOTBALL LEAGUE
JAKO

The Wasp. The Pest. Call Paul Dickov what you want, but he showed that he still had magic left in them there wee Scottish boots with his first goal since returning to the club against Fulham.

Late goals from Jimmy Bullard and Danny Murphy secured a 3-2 victory for the home side and ended Leicester's Carling Cup campaign. Meanwhile, City's fine league form continued with an emphatic 4-0 victory over Cheltenham Town at a sunny Whaddon Road.

Alliance
Leicester
C&G Cheltenham &

The Foxes bagged 10 points from a possible 12 during the month of August – sending out a statement of intent to their League One rivals. Nigel Pearson was awarded the Manager of the Month award for his side's efforts.

Leicester made their bow in the Johnstone's Paint Trophy during September,
while in League One Nigel Pearson's side were further able to build on the solid foundations they had put in place.

City's first trip of the campaign to the capital took them to the Matchroom Stadium (Brisbane Road to you and me), with the Foxes looking to bounce back from their Millwall defeat. Dave Martin was now seemingly on his way to winning the battle with Paul Henderson for the number one jersey.

Matty Fryatt grabbed his sixth goal of the campaign in the 3-1 victory over Orient – with over 2,500 City fans on hand to witness the win, as Martin Ling's men gave Leicester one of their toughest tests at that stage of the season. The Foxes moved up one place to fifth in the table.

Leicester made five changes to their side for the visit of Lincoln City in round two of the Johnstone's Paint Trophy – with Paul Henderson returning in goal. The Aussie stopper was in fine form on the night – producing two outstanding saves in the penalty shoot out after the game had ended goalless.

New recruit Bruno Berner (far left) was handed his debut against the Imps, having signed a three-year contract with the club at the beginning of the month. Youngster Craig King (third from the right) also made his City bow on the evening when entering the fray as a second half substitute.

Arsenal loanee Kerrea Gilbert enjoyed a successful start to his Leicester City career. Ever present in the league to date, the youngster took time out ahead of the 1-0 victory over Hartlepool United to thumb through the club's matchday programme.

The season reached October with fans young and old coming out in numbers to support Nigel Pearson's side, as word spread of the new and improved Foxes.

In the space of just six months the Walkers Stadium was transformed from a nervy nightmare to a melting pot of passion, pride and newfound optimism. The City faithful had picked themselves up, dusted themselves down and thrown themselves behind Nigel Pearson's men following the club's relegation.

Chairman Milan Mandaric had chosen to let his side's football do the talking during the early part of the season, but here he is seen speaking to *BBC East Midlands Today* reporter Natalie Jackson ahead of the club's local derby against Northampton Town.

JAKO
25

City went into their fixture against the Cobblers well in the mix at the top of the League One table. The Foxes sat in fourth position going into the clash – just four points behind table toppers Scunthorpe United with a game in hand.

The Northampton Town fixture was chosen as the date of the club's annual Remembrance Day activities. Squadron Leader Jim Vince expertly landed the RAF Squirrel helicopter safely inside the stadium before Chris Smith of Sixty Squadron at Shaftsbury delivered the matchball.

The tunring point? Nigel Pearson found it impossible to hide his disappointment following his side's 3-2 reverse at Brighton & Hove Albion. The Foxes had raced in to a 2-0 lead, only to see the Seagulls, then mastered by former City boss Micky Adams, stage an incredible second half comeback.

November began with a bang, but could City maintain their outstanding early season form?

City fans showed their appreciation for former great John Sjoberg through a minute's applause ahead of the Bristol Rovers fixture. A stalwart of over 400 appearance, John lost his battle against illness on Thursday, October 2 2008 at the age of 67.

LEIC
JAKO
Tiles

Can one decision change a season? Few would have raised an eyebrow when Barry Hayles was introduced in place of Steve Howard with 66 minutes played. The Foxes were a goal down at the time and looked to be heading to consecutive league defeats. But Hayles had other ideas as he came on to spark a revival.

While the Walkers Stadium attendances had remained pretty consistent with that which the club had enjoyed in the Championship, the same could not be said for the club's press box, with numbers roughly halved due to the coverage of the division at national newspaper level.

November proved to be the busiest month of the season, with eight matches in total, including fixtures against Yeovil Town, Stevenage Borough and Dagenham & Redbridge for the first time in the club's history.

Due to their new divisional status, the Foxes found themselves in the opening round of the FA Cup for the first time in their history. However, the fans took it all in their stride, enjoying entertaining victories over both the Daggers and the Boro.

City travelled to Swindon Town sitting proudly at the top of the division. The Foxes looked to be coasting to victory – with goals from Matt Oakley and Matty Fryatt sending them into the closing stages with a 2-0 lead. However, late strikes from Simon Cox and Barry Corr earned the home side a share of the spoils.

December and Christmas: traditionally a time for giving, but Nigel Pearson certainly didn't think so. The Foxes began the month at the top of the tree.

Local hero and Foxes fan Rendall Monroe returned from his latest title defence to parade his European Super Bantamweight belt ahead of the Peterborough clash.

Not content with holding the accolade for the fastest ever goal scored by a City player, Matty Fryatt had historians scrambling for their record books once again when he hit back-to-back hat-tricks against Dagenham & Redbridge and Southend United – the first City player to do so for 83 years.

City's first trip to Brunton Park since 1983 saw them register a battling 2-1 victory over Carlisle United. Manager Nigel Pearson, returning to the club that he had managed 10 years prior, praised his side's 'staying power' following the game – City fought back from a goal down.

CARLISLE UNITED
Premier
Stobart
Stobart

JAKO
JAKO
KO

Matty Fryatt is strapped up for action by assistant physio Tom Freeman ahead of City's crunch clash against in-form Peterborough United. Darren Ferguson's men went in to the game on the back of a 14-match unbeaten run, but were demolished 4-0 by the rampant Foxes.

Italian Team Uniforms
paddypower

Matt Oakley wheels away in delight after giving the Foxes the lead in their Boxing Day clash against Leeds United. The game ends all square.

The fans were out in force over the festive period, with the Foxes continuing their fine run of form by remaining undefeated for the month of December.

Steve Howard displays his no-nonsense celebration following his strike in the 2-1 victory over Hereford United.

Gone are the days when the team tactics would be written on the back of a cigarette packet...
Assistant boss Steve Walsh and performance analyst Andrew Blake give the low down on the opposition to Lloyd Dyer and Mark Davies.

Matty Fryatt's goalscoring exploits in December earned him the Powerade Player of the Month award.
The striker became the first City player to score 20 goals before Christmas since Derek Doogan in 1966.

Plenty of commitment on display, but no goals to see as City's FA Cup tie with Championship side Crystal Palace ends goalless.

Amongst old friends. Paul Dickov gets a hug from Crystal Palace keeper and former team-mate Julian Speroni, as he returns from injury to line up against the Eagles.

January saw the club cement their position at the top – with victories over Leyton Orient, Huddersfield Town, Yeovil Town and Northampton Town. Only Brighton & Hove Albion were able to nick a point during the period.

Following injury to Alex Tunchev, extra responsibility was heaped on young centre-half pairing Jack Hobbs and Michael Morrison. The duo rose to the task with style, grabbing a goal apiece in the 4-2 victory over Huddersfield Town.

Seeing double? Referee Craig Pawson deemed that Brighton's away strip clashed with City's home colours when Albion visited the Walkers Stadium in January. The visitors were forced to don Leicester's third kit on the evening, although they were still able to battle out a hard-fought 0-0 draw.

Max Gradel decided to brighten up the gloomy conditions in the winter months with a pair of pink boots – much to the amusement of his team-mates.

The cold snap was good news for some. With Foxes fans quick to don Leicester City hats, scarves and gloves – the City Megastore reporting record sales of winter paraphernalia.

Steve Howard's incredible work ethic and unselfishness went unnoticed in some quarters, but his presence and strength were on show for all to see when Leicester fought back from a goal down to dispatch Northampton Town 2-1 at Sixfields.

Tom Cleverley arrived at the club on loan from Manchester United following the departure of Mark Davies to Bolton Wanderers and quietly went about his business before exploding on to the scene against Northampton.

Club Plummer Terry Prince, Head Groundsman Ed Mowe and Club Electrian Matt Greaves were handed the arduous task of removing the snow from the surrounding areas of the ground ahead of the live televised clash against Oldham Athletic.

Judging by this picture, it is hard to believe that a couple of hours prior Matty Fryatt had not been expected to play. Physio Dave Rennie recalled. “After 90 minutes of manipulation with were able to get him out on the pitch.” Fryatt grabbed the first goal in a comfortable 4-1 victory at Walsall.

Emergency keeper. More like seasoned shot stopper. Dean Windass took over in goal when Oldham came to the Walkers Stadium without a replacement goalkeeper.

Andy King went from strength to strength as the season progressed. Seen here in battle in the 1-1 all home draw with Swindon Town, the midfielder could boast the proud record of having started every game until this point – scoring a respectable 11 goals during the process.

They once loved him in Hartlepool. The locals have fond memories of his playing days at Victoria Park, but they have been sick of the sight of the big striker ever since. Steve Howard took his tally of goals against his former club to ten, with a brace in this hard-fought 2-2 draw.

It always pays to do your homework. Mark Bunn save's Ricky Lambert's penalty. Bunn explained he had studied Lambert's previous penalty kicks before the game with goalkeeping coach Mike Stowell. The result meant the Foxes had managed to go 20 league games without defeat – a new club record.

AWAY SUPPORTERS
SOUTH STAND
EMERGENCY EXIT
EXIT
Topps Tiles

The sun poked out from behind the clouds for the first time in 2009 to witness City's 1-0 victory at the Memorial Stadium.

A 25-yard free-kick, five minutes into injury time at Milton Keynes. Fast forward a split second and the ball was hitting the back of the net. Later Max Gradel chose to shun the media spotlight to relay the news to his friends and family back in his homeland.

JAKO
Coca-Cola FOOTBALL LEAGUE
4
22
8

A young fan shows her support during the Stockport County clash.

March saw City's incredible run of unbeaten games come to an end at Tranmere, but the support from the stands never wavered.

All sides equal. City's matchday programme took on a retro-style square format for the campaign, similar to the one used by the club in the 1970s.

Matty Fryatt looks to the skies on a treacherous evening at the Walkers Stadium.
The game against Stockport County finished 1-1 with former Fox Chris O'Grady grabbing the goal for the visitors.

City turned on the style when they faced Cheltenham Town and registered a 4-0 victory against the table's bottom side – and it could have been more. Matty Fryatt was one of the scorers, but it was Matt Oakley's goal that was judged by many as City's Goal of the Season.

An unhappy return. Former City boss Martin Allen took over the managerial reins at Whaddon Road in September, following in the footsteps of his father, Dennis. But despite a late rally from his side, the Robins were unable to avoid the drop.

The many faces of management. City manager Nigel Pearson shares a joke with the assistant referee during the home draw with Colchester United.

A week earlier at the New Den Pearson saluted the Foxes faithful following his side's crucial 1-0 victory over Millwall.

New blue shoes for Max Gradel; while Paul Dickov waves goodbye to the injury blues. He finally draws a line under his woes by bagging City's only goal of the game in their 1-1 draw with the resurgent Colchester United.

Four seasons on the day, but City can't quite hit the right notes on the field of play.
However, there were no excuses from Nigel Pearson and his side, who were resoundedly beaten 2-0 at Peterborough .

A mysterious member of the backroom team. City's Sports Science intern Matt Reeves captures the action, before the footage is then reviewed and scrutinised following the match as the Foxes continue with their 'no stone unturned' approach to the game.

Young mascot Olivia led the Foxes out onto the pitch for their League One encounter against Carlisle United.

When all around you are losing their heads.... Panic never quite set in amongst the supporters, but there were certainly one or two jitters. However, win, lose or draw Nigel Pearson remained a rock throughout the campaign.

Matty Fryatt climbs above the Carlisle defence to score a rare headed goal with just three minutes of the contest remaining...

...and thinks he's secured all three points, but there is a further twist as Carlisle level. Peterborough's 2-1 win at Oldham cuts the lead at the top to two points.

Up, up and away! After going a goal behind to Hereford United at Edgar Street, City's class eventually took its toll. Lloyd Dyer was on hand to pick up the pieces after Steve Howard had seen his effort saved to put the Foxes 2-1 ahead with just 16 minutes of the game remaining.

Second half substitute and fans' favourite Max Gradel shows his appreciation to the 2,000 travelling supporters following the 3-1 victory.

City fans had certainly enjoyed life on the road throughout the season. The victory at Hereford was their 12th away win of the campaign...

...and left the Foxes 10-points clear of third places Millwall with just four games of the season left to play.

Paul Hing opened up the proceedings for the visit of Leeds United with a rendition of the Post Horn Gallop.
Paul, a lifelong City fan, was tutored by former Gallop man Henry Shipley in his younger years.

Wayne Brown, who had joined the club on loan from Hull City in January following the season ending injury to Alex Tunchev, became a firm favourite with the City fans with a string of no-nonsense displays at the middle of the Foxes defence, as Leeds striker Luciano Becchio finds out.

Nearly there! Steve Howard out-jumps the Leeds United defence with a skyscraper leap and heads the ball home to secure all three points with just seconds of the game remaining.

JAKO
Topps Tiles
LCFC

Millwall's 2-0 victory over Peterborough later that day meant that the City fans travelled to Roots Hall knowing that victory would secure the title.

Chief Executive Lee Hoos and Chairman Milan Mandaric looked relaxed before the game, but the picture doesn't tell the story. The City coach had been delayed in traffic on the way to the ground. The pre-match news also confirmed that Steve Howard would have to miss the contest through illness.

It was all smiles in the away end, as Matty Fryatt gave the Foxes the lead from the penalty spot against the Shrimpers, before pouncing on Lloyd Dyer's crossbar-rattling free-kick to take his personal tally to five for the season against the Essex outfit.

Topps Tiles
JAKO
LCFC
12

Job done. Victory secured promotion back to the Championship at the first attempt.

City Chairman Milan Mandaric was quick to praise the achievements of Nigel Pearson, his coaching staff and players shortly after the final whistle.

Party time on the pitch...

...and in the stands

JAKO
27
31

Matty Fryatt can't contain his jubilation, while left, the City squad show their appreciation to the travelling support.

In a moment of calm, Nigel Pearson congratulates his players for their hard work during the season in the dressing room after the game. However, the City boss was quick to remind his players that he fully expected his side to go out and win their final two games of the campaign...

...before taking time out to celebrate with his backroom staff.

DAVID
Coca-Cola
FOOTBALL LEAGUE

Alan Birchenall kicked off the celebrations by completing his annual charity run ahead of the Scunthorpe United fixture. Seen here with his son Dean, The Birch has worked tirelessly for local organisations over the years, raising in excess of £750,000. A week later he was awarded the Freedom of the City of Leicester.

Manager Nigel Pearson and Chairman Milan Mandaric acknowledge the Walkers Stadium crowd, before Matt Oakley lifts the League One trophy...

MPIONS
Coca-Cola
FOOTBALL
LEAGUE

More than a bottle of pop. The trophy which confirms City's return to the Championship is made from sterling silver and gold plate and symbolises a Coke bottle.

LEICESTER CITY F.C.
CHAMPIONS

Andy King, Kerrea Gilbert, Matty Fryatt and two goal hero on the night Michael Morrison get their hands on City's first piece of silverware since they won the League Cup in 2000.

A beaming Bruno Berner holds aloft the trophy.

The trophy is in safe hands with Dave Stockdale and Tony Warner, who spent time on loan with City from Fulham and Hull City.

Home grown. Max Gradel and Andy King were two of eight Leicester City Academy graduates who represented the club during the campaign.

Smile please. Captain Matt Oakley and Manager Nigel Pearson show off the League One trophy to the assembled press pack following the game.

JAKO
Coca-Cola

City unveiled their 2009-11 home kit ahead of the Scunthorpe fixture. The new shirt will not carry a sponsor in recognition of the club's 125th anniversary.

Thumbs the word.... Nigel Pearson gestures to the crowd following the Crewe fixture.

With the championship won and the League One trophy safely in the cabinet, the fans were in celebratory mood for the trip to Crewe Alexandra. After tucking in at the famous local fish and chip shop, the Blue Army simply enjoyed their day out at the Alexandra Stadium.

Despite their relegation to League Two, the Alex played their part in what was a memorable day for all those that attended. The Cheshire club were perfect hosts for City's special day, with their players performing a guard of honour to welcome the champions on to the pitch ahead of the game.

League One final table

	P	W	D	L	F	A	W	D	L	F	A	Pts	GD
Leicester City	**46**	**13**	**9**	**1**	**41**	**16**	**14**	**6**	**3**	**43**	**23**	**96**	**+45**
Peterborough United	46	14	6	3	41	22	12	5	6	37	32	89	+24
MK Dons	46	12	4	7	42	25	14	5	4	41	22	87	+36
Leeds United	46	17	2	4	49	20	9	4	10	28	29	84	+28
Millwall	46	13	4	6	30	21	12	3	8	33	32	82	+10
Scunthorpe United	46	13	5	5	44	24	9	5	9	38	39	76	+19
Tranmere Rovers	46	15	5	3	41	20	6	6	11	21	29	74	+13
Southend United	46	13	2	8	29	20	8	6	9	29	41	71	-3
Huddersfield Town	46	9	8	6	32	28	9	6	8	30	37	68	-3
Oldham Athletic	46	9	9	5	35	24	7	8	8	31	41	65	+1
Bristol Rovers	46	11	4	8	44	29	6	8	9	35	32	63	+18
Colchester United	46	7	4	12	21	24	11	5	7	37	34	63	0
Walsall	46	10	3	10	34	36	7	7	9	27	30	61	-5
Leyton Orient	46	6	6	11	24	33	9	5	9	21	24	56	-12
Swindon Town	46	8	7	8	37	34	4	10	9	31	37	53	-3
Brighton & Hove Albion	46	6	6	11	32	40	7	7	9	23	30	52	-15
Yeovil Town	46	6	10	7	26	29	6	5	12	15	37	51	-25
Stockport County	46	9	7	7	34	28	7	5	11	25	29	50	+2
Hartlepool United	46	8	7	8	45	40	5	4	14	21	39	50	-13
Carlisle United	46	8	7	8	36	32	4	7	12	20	37	50	-13
Northampton Town	46	8	8	7	38	29	4	5	14	23	36	49	-4
Crewe Alexandra	46	8	4	11	30	38	4	6	13	29	44	46	-23
Cheltenham Town	46	7	6	10	30	38	2	6	15	21	53	39	-40
Hereford United	46	6	4	13	23	28	3	3	17	19	51	34	-37

League One results

August

Sat	9	H	MK Dons	L1	W	2-0	23,351
Tue	12	H	Stockport County	LC	W	1-0	7,386
Sat	16	A	Stockport County	L1	D	0-0	7,151
Sat	23	H	Tranmere Rovers	L1	W	3-1	17,798
Wed	27	A	Fulham	LC	L	2-3	7,584
Sat	30	A	Cheltenham Town	L1	W	4-0	5,344

September

Tue	2	A	Hartlepool United	JPT	W	3-0	2,807
Sat	13	H	Millwall	L1	L	0-1	19,591
Sat	20	A	Leyton Orient	L1	W	3-1	6,448
Tue	23	H	Lincoln City	JPT	W	0-0 (3-1 on pens)	8,046
Sat	27	H	Hartlepool United	L1	W	1-0	18,578
Tue	30	A	Colchester United	L1	W	1-0	5,133

October

Sat	4	A	Huddersfield Town	L1	W	3-2	16,212
Sat	18	A	Oldham Athletic	L1	D	1-1	8,901
Tue	21	H	Walsall	L1	D	2-2	17,178
Sat	25	H	Northampton Town	L1	D	0-0	22,795
Tue	28	A	Brighton & Hove Albion	L1	L	2-3	6,282

November

Sat	1	H	Bristol Rovers	L1	W	2-1	18,941
Tue	4	A	Rotherham United	JPT	L	0-2	4,255
Sat	8	H	Stevenage Borough	FAC	W	3-0	7,586
Tue	11	H	Yeovil Town	L1	W	1-0	16,528
Sat	15	A	Swindon Town	L1	D	2-2	9,499
Sat	22	A	Scunthorpe United	L1	W	2-1	7,967
Tue	25	H	Crewe Alexandra	L1	W	2-1	16,961
Sat	29	H	Dagenham & Redbridge	FAC	W	3-2	7,791

December

Sat	6	H	Southend United	L1	W	3-0	16,836
Sat	13	A	Carlisle United	L1	W	2-1	7,085
Sat	20	H	Peterborough United	L1	W	4-0	23,390
Fri	26	A	Leeds United	L1	D	1-1	27,507
Sun	28	H	Hereford United	L1	W	2-1	22,920

January

Sat	3	H	Crystal Palace	FAC	D	0-0	15,976
Sat	10	H	Leyton Orient	L1	W	3-0	18,240
Wed	14	A	Crystal Palace	FAC	L	1-2	6,023
Mon	19	A	Yeovil Town	L1	W	2-0	4,569
Sat	24	H	Huddersfield Town	L1	W	4-2	21,311
Tue	27	H	Brighton & Hove Albion	L1	D	0-0	17,410
Sat	31	A	Northampton Town	L1	W	2-1	7,028

February

Tue	3	A	Walsall	L1	W	4-1	5,634
Sat	7	H	Oldham Ahtletic	L1	D	0-0	22,328
Sat	14	H	Swindon Town	L1	D	1-1	19,926
Tue	17	A	Hartlepool United	L1	D	2-2	4,068
Sat	21	A	Bristol Rovers	L1	W	1-0	9,138
Sat	28	A	MK Dons	L1	D	2-2	17,717

March

Tue	3	H	Stockport County	L1	D	1-1	16,378
Sat	7	H	Cheltenham Town	L1	W	4-0	18,939
Wed	11	A	Tranmere Rovers	L1	L	0-2	6,032
Sat	14	A	Millwall	L1	W	1-0	13,261
Sat	21	H	Colchester United	L1	D	1-1	20,218
Sat	28	A	Peterborough United	L1	L	0-2	14,110

April

Sat	4	H	Carlisle United	L1	D	2-2	20,159
Sat	11	A	Hereford United	L1	W	3-1	4,389
Mon	13	H	Leeds United	L1	W	1-0	25,507
Sat	18	A	Southend United	L1	W	2-0	10,089
Fri	24	H	Scunthorpe United	L1	D	2-2	30,542

May

Sat	2	A	Crewe Alexandra	L1	W	3-0	6,982

Epilogue by Neil Plumb

Relegation was a bitter pill to swallow for me, like all City fans. In our worst nightmares we had never drempt of third tier football. With a world class stadium and the backing of the Chairman all our thoughts were of getting back to the Premier League - where we all believe we belong.

In July 2008 I was handed the honour of photographing and documenting such a historic season for the club only months after setting up my own business. It would be a chance for me to make new friends and chalk off some grounds that realistically, as a City supporter, we never contemplated visiting in the League. What would the grounds be like? Would the team be able to cope with small, tight atmospheres? Would the players really fancy a midweek trip to Hartlepool or the long trip to Carlisle?

It became clear after just a couple of games that the Blue Army were going to embrace, enjoy and party their way through the cold nights, long drives and mediocre facilities to play their part in a special time.

On the pitch, things were looking positive. New signings Jack Hobbs, Lloyd Dyer and Alex Tunchev were a statement of intent. A new manager seemed to have put a smile back on the players' faces - players who had looked so forlorn just a few months earlier. Matty Fryatt, Matt Oakley and Steve Howard were all looking sharp and ready for the challenge ahead.

This book is a small snapshot into a memorable season. We won't forget in a hurry those great away days at Cheltenham, Millwall, Bristol Rovers, Hereford and Southend. A late, late Steve Howard goal against Leeds , the thumping of Peterborough and the fantastic trophy presentation all made the Walkers Stadium a place to go and enjoy football again.

I hope you enjoy reliving the season through this book as much as I enjoyed capturing every moment during such a memorable season.

I'd like to dedicate this book to Anna and Eve and all my family. Big thanks must also go to Darren Cresswell , Alex Hannam and Jon Sanders plus all the Leicester City staff , players and management for their help and support, without which this book would not have been possible.

Here's to another promotion challenge. Blue Army!